SUNDANCES

Prose Poems

Other works by William Sun:

The Blue (Fiction 2013)
River Sanctuary Publishing

SUNDANCES

Prose Poems

William Climbing Sun

SUNDANCES
Copyright © 2017 by William Sun

All rights reserved. No part of this book may be reproduced, stored in a retrieval system, or transmitted, in any form or by any means, electronic, mechanical, photocopying, recording, or otherwise, without the written prior permission of the author, except in the case of brief quotations embodied in critical articles and reviews.

Cover Design by River Sanctuary Graphic Arts

ISBN 978-1-935914-55-6

Printed in the United States of America

Additional copies are available from:
www.riversanctuarypublishing.com
Amazon.com

RIVER SANCTUARY PUBLISHING
P.O Box 1561
Felton, CA 95018
www.riversanctuarypublishing.com
Dedicated to the awakening of the New Earth

Acknowledgments

The episodes related in this book span the better part of a lifetime. Even though childhood in general is an altered state, and even though my own upbringing was the opposite of ideal—let alone blissful—the early years are at bottom an astonishing segment in a life. A slow observer and learner, it did not begin to become consciously apparent to me until my mid-twenties that there is magic afoot on our earth—not to mention the entire Cosmos. So my first expression of most profound gratitude goes out to our beautiful planet and the Intelligence responsible for its conception, creation, continuing resilience, and persistent, effulgent beauty.

Carol Sun, my wife and partner of well over three decades, has left her imprint throughout these pages by bringing a blend of wild yet lighthearted enchantment to our day-to-day life out of which this offering was allowed to flourish.

I am exceedingly indebted to Katherine Zeigler for her insightful, labor-of-love editing skill that gently steered me toward a clearer, more all-embracing manuscript than I would have produced if my verses were left to ricochet off the inside surface of my own bubble.

Expert publisher, unselfish editor, and general motivator Annie Elizabeth Porter's unwavering support, patience, and generosity fostered the psychic atmosphere which allowed these poems to be birthed onto paper when their optimal moment had arrived.

Those individuals—known and unknown, heralded and unheralded—who appear as integral players in these episodes are to be acknowledged for their contribution to the wonders, trials, and evolution of the author and are granted his deepest appreciation.

Lastly, to those friends, family members, acquaintances, co-conspirators, and innocent bystanders who have been asked to comment on these musings, accept my wish that you be rewarded in kind for your selflessness.

Contents

Introduction	1
Saint Ann's Sound	3
Racing Native	5
Lynne's Flight	7
Lifetime Wave	9
Climbing Sun	11
The Canyon Bust	13
Yours in Black Elk	16
Moment at Kaupo Church	20
Midnight Massive Meditation	22
Synchronous All Over Again	25
At the Stoplight	27
American Bridge	28
Moon Party at Last Chance Road	30
Up Shasta	32
Girl in Charge of Joy	36
Daughters	41
Sweat Without End	44
Stop the Musical	46
Freeway Scream	48
Kaiser Pass Primal Love	50
Rebirth by Fire	52
The Great Image Heist	54
Presence Circle	58

Over New Mexico	60
Celestial Timing	62
Being on the Gurney	65
Mile 232 Rapid	66
The Adoption	68
Twenty Fourteen Doesn't Speak—It Rages	69
The Grandkids	72
Me Rilke Angels	74

Introduction

Through the ages, the Sundance, a Native American ritual, has brought thousands of souls into a rich parallel realm by providing a safe, guided environment where they could profoundly experience their humanity. The ritual includes a wide spectrum of sacred stimulants such as facing extreme weather, undergoing skin piercing, and embracing uninterrupted rhythmic motion around a pole to ancient chants and the pulse of the drum—all while fasting. The dancer performs this feat in a deep state of prayer for the benefit of family and larger community. Every known human emotion is not only experienced but amplified or laid bare. The end result is a journey into the mystical realm. Non-Indians are not permitted to witness the ceremony in order to maintain its cultural purity.

Especially in the culture of America outside of the original Natives, there is an inherent—often suppressed—longing for connection to the North American landforms and water bodies with which we interact. For those who have traveled beyond the continent, this reverence for the larger planet likely lives within us as well, however prominent or dormant. Here then is one soul's alternate set of lenses through which to view our continent and our world. A fabric of deeply human adventures to more clearly appreciate the intricacies, the enchantments, and the inner and outer intensities presented with the intention to ultimately make all our journeys more self-revered.

In the following pages, through this collection of synchronistic and/or highly-charged emotional escapades, my intent is that you find corollaries to your own encounters with the Great Mystery. Perhaps these have been forgotten or filed away for later consumption—or suppressed as too painful, too crazy-making, too indulgent to examine, and certainly too risky to share. It is not out of the question for the person we have become to revisit the person we once were and re-imagine, re-enliven, even validate or restore that being.

This perhaps can be our offering, our prayer, our healing, our form of sundance: to more deeply appreciate ourselves, honor our families, enrich our communities, and benefit the larger world society as renewed citizens whose mission may be simply to facilitate the communication between the earthly and heavenly realms.

Saint Ann's Sound

Growing up in Catholic school in the 1950's was nothing short of otherworldly. No one could escape the alluring aura of Latin. When sung repeatedly, the intrinsic poetry submerged within it, released. I swear its allure surfaced onto our pre-adolescent psychic complexions. It even enhanced our class pictures. Certain of us became tenderly addicted.

We became saturated in ancient vats of Gregorian chant. Simply droning the *Litany of the Saints* was a peak immersion—a re-baptizing in the tears of wild yet holy ecstatics and brutalized martyrs all through history. We swam in pools of *Gloria's*, *Kyrie's* and *Hosanna's*. Harmonies sprang from us effortlessly. Without warning, we fell in deep love with long vowel sounds.

A choir boy at my first Christmas-eve midnight mass, I somersaulted slowly through a vast harmonic ether like an enraptured, pint-sized monk. And wanted more. Tucked at the rear of the apse behind the altar, resonance displaced who we had been. Heart-shaped sounds issued from our mouths, ricocheted off the parabolic surfaces and eddied about us like holy water before swilling about in the packed church. I'm certain the congregation never knew what hit them.

I have since come to know that such luscious terrestrial occurrences are for all practical purposes, God revealing

Godself—or to use the Catholic vernacular, the Holy-Spirit-Presence aspect of the Most High.

The exalted state that dwells in this eddy has never left me. For months and years at a time I would be the one to leave "IT". And just when I'd been sufficiently numbed by the grinding of life's gears, I would arrive at some parched crossroad where IT had likely been waiting for eternity to welcome me. What I know is IT is ever available, and always issues from the same vastness that lurked in that apse.

Sages say a good question is more illuminating than a good answer: If God is an equal-opportunity Arranger, does it not follow that—even though our adult ears get distracted from the background alleluias of their childhood—the nature of every person, animal and thing must be, at its core, one of sonorous exultation?

Racing Native

There were few wild places in and around the town of my youth. The environs felt outwardly and inwardly flat. Virtually everything had been touched by the hand—more often the fist or knife—of man. And it is fact: ninety-nine percent of Ohio is disturbed.

But one place in my neighborhood seemed ever wild, an ornately-fenced grove of giant trees where President Hayes lived out his days. His house and adjoining museum perched above a rare, pristine, wooded hillside I fell in love with. Half park, half wild, the slope always beckoned and I usually answered.

The adjacent museum overflowed with artifacts connected to the long-dead president residing there in the ground, under the maples and oaks, next to his wife and horse. His collection of baskets, arrows, leggings, beadwork, war hammers, quilts and paintings of noble red people were displayed in abundance, juxtaposed with his war uniforms and presidential paraphernalia. This sea of objects spun through my prepubescent brain like a carousel of living history. One whiff of the old leather, wood, and cloth in there and without knowing it I'd begin to daydream back into that earlier time.

One summer, word circulated among us kids that the land on the slope was the same now as it was when only Indians lived there. There were remnants of a trail they had used and a spring where they had collected water. One friend said he thought he'd caught a glimpse of a squaw the day before. He saw her and blinked a long blink, but by then she'd vanished.

For days I was scared to pass through the iron gates and go back inside the grove. Its century-old trees by themselves were an intimidating presence. My susceptible, God-fearing self wasn't prepared to meet someone from another time let alone another culture. What if I were drawn in? Forced to skin hides or bury dead braves? Made to dance around naked?

In the end, my hillside beckoned me like a jilted, insistent lover. So I summoned up some nerve and rode my bicycle in there, thinking I could make a fast getaway if I were chased. I'd only recently taught myself to ride and was still learning both the machine and the newfound freedom it afforded.

As I neared the slope, it didn't take long for the air to go blurry and behave like a rippling transparent curtain. I peered through it into another dimension where there were only feelings. I felt an Indian brave going about his business. I could sense myself merging with his large, enticing energy field. I intuited he was going to notice me so I raced away on my bicycle. As I sped around the side of the museum it seemed safe to glance back. I slammed into the open tailgate of a parked pickup truck full of gravel. I might have killed myself.

I swear I heard laughter.

Lynne's Flight

Lynne was the college love of my life. Our time together was not unlike a drag race: a burning-rubber start; a surreal glide so smooth the deceptive speed was a dream-inducing sedative; a deployed-parachute deceleration; a final and irreversible crash into the finish line.

I spent my last pre-graduate summer in northern Ohio as a junior bridge engineer. In late August, Lynne was visiting from Miami Shores for ten days. We had our standard love trance going with all the mutual delight to which young lovers claim entitlement.

The roar of our relationship's engine seemed so glorious I missed every kicked-up stone angrily poking holes in the undercarriage of our hot rod: my subtle force-feeding of Grandma's indigestible Vatican fare which gave Lynne the dry heaves; my entitlement to her body and playful mind causing me to take her for granted; all the above converging to slam our dragster into a wall two adult lifetimes before the finish line.

Even at the airport all seemed well. We hugged and kissed passionately vowing that in a mere two weeks we would be back in each other's arms in the embrace of the Florida heat. And then on to the blissful afterlife of professional togetherness. We would become our own eternal pit stop.

I hung around to watch the takeoff. As her plane entered the sky, this non-visible, almost-tactile wave from the jet's slipstream rippled through me. "It is over," it murmured. How could I know something that arbitrary? My dashboard dismissed the paranormal transmission but my feral body did a wheelstand in resonance with a tragic Smoky Robinson song with which we were obsessed: *Just a Mirage*.

The day I got back to school she confirmed the crash. "We're trying to drive this coupe on the wrong fuel over glass, nails and black ice," she essentially said. It took years before I was willing to surrender to sweet speed like that again.

Lifetime Wave

The paddleout is always a prayer. Work the upper arms. Welcome the salt spray into the lungs and over the back. Invite the base note built into the waves to reverberate through body and brain.

This morning's prayer is longer than any other. After an epic yet enlivening exertion, I get past the break line by stroking for my life up the face of an impending blue-green mountain. I leave the roar behind and spin around only to gasp in disbelief. The features on the coast are barely visible. Palm trees look like blades of grass. It feels like I'm hovered over the very edge of the continental shelf. This is not just new territory. At a solid quarter mile offshore, it's a brave new universe.

I dwell here on the ocean bluff thirty feet from A1A, the premier scenic north-south route that links all the spits and islets of sand along the eastern beaches of the Sunshine State. This is my home turf. I've spent part of every day for three years in the sweet seawater out my back door. Sometimes all day. So like any other morning graced with waves, I wax my board and head out like an innocent with no clue what savagery is surging just over the horizon.

What I don't know is this groundswell is being spawned from a low-grade hurricane paralleling Florida's east coast. If I were able to settle into the magnitude of this planetary blessing, if I were able to translate the language of this perfect tropical disturbance, I would have to overstay my welcome out here. But I am drunk because the night wind has vanished into a dynamic stillness punctuated by these immense sets that feel like they're here because the earth is coming apart. It's the final day of September 1971. I leave for Oregon in three hours. If I live to board the plane.

I let one set go. If I let another pass I'll psyche myself into paralysis. I go into no mind at the next approach. (I can only know this after the fact. If I were in charge of my mind, I'd never have challenged this monstrous manifestation of liquid matter.) In a scant second, I'm a lone joker merging with an oversize freak. A marriage no doubt conceived when God was daydreaming while designing deserts to match the stark stillness of Mercury.

I sense the acceleration, stand erect and drop in backside left as if playing in a common three-foot wind swell. But this descent is akin to sledding down a steep childhood slope. Except this hill is exploding into white mayhem at my back. Leashes on surfboards have yet to be invented.

Long after the bottom turn, I'm a stray bullet suddenly engulfed by a chamber. The thing has tubed over and licks at my scalp—admiring itself through me. I emerge through a sunlit portal, the screaming embodiment of joy immersed in a birthday present for the ages.

Climbing Sun

Florida is a receding dream. The Poseidon Nuclear Missile tracking system I helped birth is behind me. Selling my soul for a draft deferment is over. Two mates and I cross the country bound for Hawaii with only backpacks, hammocks, and surfboards to reclaim said soul.

We camp a night in Texas. Next morning while we paint a yin-yang symbol on the hood of our ailing micro-sedan, the cops drop by to ask us what the hell we are up to. "Heaven!" we reply. They consider arresting us.

We stop pushing our luck and drive nonstop to San Diego. Realizing the shape of our east-coast surf sticks won't cut it in Hawaii, we sell them and the sedan to some surf-shop owners for a hundred fifty bucks. Seventy-five of that is the car.

The following afternoon we land in Honolulu. A friend of a friend picks us up. On the way over the pali to Kailua, we get run off the freeway by some locals. The cops tell them they shouldn't do that, even if we are there to steal their waves.

A couple days later we hitch out to the North Shore and discover a World War II Army bunker embedded in the mountain above Pipeline. We sweet talk the neighbor, hang our hammocks, and move in.

The more spiritually advanced California surf brothers in the shack at the bottom of the trail turn us onto duck eggs, fasting, and the book, *The Impersonal Life*. We go all in for macrobiotic feasts over campfires.

Early one Sunday morning, I thumb out toward an abandoned macadamia nut grove to break my three-day fast. I walk a long mile on a red dirt road. Sugar cane towers on both sides. The wind makes music with it. The crisp morning drenches my skin. Seeps into my spirit.

The sun climbs through a glorious azure sky. I stop. "The sun is climbing…The sun is climbing…Climbing Sun! "When I hear myself say it, I shudder. And stammer, "Me?…No way… Not gonna call myself that."

But California has other plans. There I have to dust the name off—after Hawaii teaches me all it can—or become just another average Joe in the richer landscape of peers with customized handles. Why not become instead the sun-crazed, swaying-on-the-ledge, test-the-outer-reaches-of-convention researcher? Why not invite instant conversation, ego-crushing judgment, even occasional kudos for courage? Why not be constantly re-infused with the spirit of that Hawaiian Sunday-morning magic? Use it for constant rebirth. Use it for fuel. And every time it's spoken, above all, use it to wake up, saddle up, and climb the omnipresent mountain. In brightness.

The Canyon Bust

The Hare Krishna's almost spear my travelling partner and me with their arsenal of spiritual weapons: breakfast, chanting, lunch, lectures, more chanting, dinner. It could only have been grace that guided us to escape their snares for a less confining enclave at the bottom of majestic Waimea Canyon.

We agree on the best spring. Dig a hole for cool storage in the damp, rocky ground. Track the wild horses to their haunts. Approach them with sweets in outstretched hands. Spend nights choosing names for them which echo their spirit: Shaddowfax; Sparkler; Brown Eyed Girl. Spend days collecting and lugging their manure to compost it for the garden. Plant everything from bush beans to scallions. The radishes are coming up.

We are squatters on Hawaii State Forest land. We tiptoe around the ruins of an ancient village. Lounge in natural whirlpools on the Waimea River's upper tributaries. Map out groves of guava and avocado, thickets of lilikoi. We brew yogurt and refrigerate it in jars on the river bottom.

This morning brings another raging Kauai backcountry extravaganza. A playful sun files the surface of our skin. Red cardinals sit on branches decreeing all is right in the world. Mynahs click and screech like broken telegraphs. Thrushes laugh at an ever-recurring punch line. Kukui trees drop their nuts like semicolons. Woodpeckers nod off in the canopy after their all-night percussion party. Walls of wild ginger send out their scent like scouts. Kamani leaves wrestle with the wind and lose.

A couple joins us from downstream. The four of us sit on rocks in the Waimea River next to our rustic hut deep into our counter-culture paperbacks. *Siddhartha. The Greening of America. Great Upon the Mountain.* The music of the stream has hypnotized us into another dimension. We no longer consider ourselves part of the mainland madness. The mad sprint for the brass ring. The neurotic concerns of urban dwellers. Instead we treasure the quiet inner joy only prolonged immersion in nature brings.

"Hey you haoles! Come out of the river now! Put your clothes on!"

Five large and armed Hawaiian police, sweating hard from their hike upriver, handcuff and march us two miles downstream to a waiting flatbed. At the station it's mug shots and off-handed remarks. "You gon' pay big fine. You gon' stay nice and warm in da slammer." We tell them about the many large bags of trash we collected and hauled out during our food runs. The guiding of lost hikers. The head count of the wild herd.

The big-cheese overseer waives jail time and fines if we will return to the canyon only to erase our traces. Leave no hint of our heaven. Wipe away our idealism. Burn the hut.

We stare into the flames and realize the whole deal is a lesson in dichotomies: the never-to-be harvested garden, the river's constant song, the yogurt souring on the river bottom, the gyrating plastic, the perfumed groves of rotting guava, the distant whinny of the skittish herd, the sweet sting of lilikoi on the tongue.

But what emerges most indelibly is the knowledge that paradise is transitory. And the sweet insight that this, and every, once-cherished Eden shall remain forever in residence behind our closed eyes.

Yours in Black Elk

We were not your typical drinking buddies in high school.

To enhance our weekends, on select Fridays, we'd hit the library for clues to solve the mystery of the whereabouts of the grave of Seneca John. John was a local northwestern Ohio chief who died under a cloud of frontier intrigue. After dark we'd snag some brews and go prowling the countryside looking for clues that matched the vague descriptions scribbled in some pioneer's journal and later distilled into some scholar's research.

One moonless night, along a back road, we zigzagged around a forbidding gully. Our game suddenly felt too real. Owl hooted. Wind gusts shivered the trees. We couldn't hear him. But we could feel the chief. Drumming. Chanting. Watching.

We walked off the stage at graduation almost never to meet face-to-face again. A few months before my buddy's premature passage to the spirit world, I was back in our in town for a spontaneous visit with my sister. After a long bicycle spin around a cluster of childhood homes and haunts, I pedaled up a hill into one of the several small parks dotting the region—and noticed him exiting his truck! As we passed I said, "Mister Wise."

He snapped out of his reverie and stared perplexed at the sweating apparition before him—a corroboration that I was somehow not who I used to be. When I softly exhaled my obsolete last name he jerked his head back and squinted. We shook hands as if our pasts were in our palms and grinned inwardly. (Later, I can only attribute our default reserve to a blanket Seneca John had thrown over us.)

Too stunned myself at the moment of this happenstance, I could not bring myself to ransack the pristine past. I simply allowed myself to wonder if he would have remembered how, nine years beyond graduation and unbeknownst to me, he had tracked down my general delivery address in Maui.

Unbeknownst to him, I'd moved to the pseudo-Deep South of Florida, having done college and a three-year career in Defense to avoid getting my brains blown out in Viet Nam. Living twenty steps from the Atlantic, I'd taken up waves and Neil Young and health food and bought way into the counter culture when I wasn't designing war machines.

I was there on the edge of the swamp at the Palm Beach Pop Festival with Iron Butterfly, Janice, and the Stones when the governor rolled through in his limo and declared it a "bad trip". I was there at the Second Atlanta Festival with an eagle feather in my headband when Hendrix played the Star-Spangled Banner a couple months before he flew from nest earth. Like-minded brethren and an eccentric white witch named Sister Pat gave me more mind-altering books than I could begin to read with my exhausting war-waging, surfing, and concert-going schedule.

A book about Crazy Horse found its way into the big box I shipped to myself when I knew I was bound for the Hawaiian Islands. That box was packed the day after I'd taken an ax to my relationship with my employer on behalf of the peace and ecology symbols I'd been displaying on my person a safe distance from the defense plant.

Having digested Crazy Horses' visions led me to notice a book in a Lahaina, Maui store window about his grand-nephew Black Elk. Both of these shamans were immersed in a world I was driven to explore. The cover of *Black Elk Speaks* has a big picture of Black Elk with a feather and headband. That face on the cover stared me down twenty times through July and August, until one day I finally walked in and bought the book.

Mere minutes later, I hitched to my Post Office to find a post card from my former classmate who'd since moved to Wyoming. The picture on the front of the card was the face of the very same Black Elk I'd just eased into my pack not an hour before. Mr. Wise simply signed his brief message, "Yours in Black Elk."

In another era I'd have run for a brew to brace myself. This time I just stepped outside and locked my eyes onto the sleeping volcano that had risen from the Pacific to make this island paradise possible. Then I held up the two faces of Black Elk, summoning and savoring the inner eruption at my core.

I was at once too self-serious and too mesmerized to overhear Seneca John having a full-spirit hoot over the whole interwoven affair.

Moment at Kaupo Church

I sleep on the bosom of the dormant volcano that dominates Maui. After a night of howling winds and chilly summer rain, morning arrives like shafts of yellow hibiscus erupting from a magenta trumpet. I pack up and start down the Kaupo Gap trail.

A mile later, at the edge of what was once the shore of the cauldron, I find a thicket of wild, lime-sized Hawaiian raspberries at their most succulent peak. I add two dozen of these rubies to the oats I'd soaked in juice overnight. This break-fast richness quickens the splendor of the unfolding day.

Six plunging, jungled miles later, the desolate road that winds along the coast poses like a rugged ribbon. The August heat at sea level engulfs me. My liquids long-consumed—and with several more miles to any known water—I flirt with panic. Rather than devolve into some ungraced state of self-inflicted pity, I discover I am drunk on the immaculate fragrance billowing off the coral reef. Off the plethora of ginger, lilikoi, plumeria, mountain apple, mango. I am stoned off the omnipresent silence. Amused by my frailty. Overcome by the sacredness of the empty landscape.

This is the nature of Hawaii. There are seemingly real places where one passes through a kind of curtain beyond the normal to the Elysian realm. Where every moment imparts some form of absolute prayer. Absolute immersion. Absolute delight.

I set off toward the Seven Sacred Pools. Rather, it feels more like they move effortlessly toward me.

Within a mile an old church appears on the ocean side of the lonesome road adjacent to a weathered cemetery overflowing with flower-bedecked graves. No soul stirs on the premises. I open the front door and am struck to the marrow by the message painted on the front wall behind the altar:

IF YE SEEK ME YE SHALL FIND ME

Perhaps because laws in this "land beyond the curtain" so decree, I dare not search for water lest I dilute the impact of the message. Dare not jar the reverence. Dare not pollute the confirmation that I seek to meld with that divinity submerged in sunlight, fauna, oceans, pools, flora, and humanity at large.

This gift is of such magnitude, the remaining many miles to the pools pass as if I'm invisible wind. A dehydrated, delirious celebrant growing more grateful with each unmeasurable step. A pilgrim who knows he will reunite with liquid yet needs not lust for it. As if the island spirits themselves are guiding him to be quenched yet remain ever anchored in their addicting delirium.

"We found you," they whisper.

Midnight Massive Meditation

I'm twenty six years old. I spend my first Christmas in Santa Cruz, California with some abnormal people. We congregate just after sundown at a hideaway house in an apple orchard above the town.

The main man is a minister of sorts with a French-sounding name who remembers his past lives. There's a quiet, otherworldly dude with inch-long fingernails who looks stoned but turns out to be a con man with healing powers. There's a fallen-away, laid back Jewish couple excited to celebrate their first Christmas as new-age Christians. A meditation teacher who screens people by asking if they've ever had the experience of piloting a spacecraft. A travelling companion addicted to itching his heart chakra. A guy who the others said should take his bowl to the Himalayas and beg rather than bother them anymore. A woman who slept with a Rolling Stone. A folk singer who fell in love with C minor and went on to flirt with fame.

I read some dreadful poems one of which starts out, "We close our eyes to see the light…"

At precisely five minutes to midnight on Christmas Eve the minister guides us through a meditation. Things are going well until he suggests we ask Jesus into our hearts.

Being a compliant sort, I pry open my heart's door and repeat, in kind of manic mantra manner, " I ask you into my heart, I ask you into my heart, I ask you into my heart," which leads me—on the stroke of midnight—into some kind of inner folding. Like I've been gently kicked out of a spaceship and there is only some foreign form of nose-diving. Then a drawn-out, slow-motion somersault. Through space, through the universe. The room itself tumbling. Tumbling through what? My mind? God's mind? Pure emptiness? Same thing?

I'm a living, breathing, run-away flywheel, looking for its long-lost engine.

Maybe it is something like what Moses experienced when he was set adrift on the Nile. Maybe the minister spiked the punch with a gymnastic incantation. Maybe the space beings have brought forth a new video game. Or the dude in the corner with the inch-long fingernails is some kind of marketer of black holes and I am his first sales call. Maybe Jesus has just launched his second coming, I bumped him, and got spellbound by his fancy frankincense deodorant.

I could get chic and declare my life is now a designer funnel pouring the real me into this moment.

Or get artistic and blame the whole thing on the Muse trying out her new harp—plucking *my* heart strings.

Or accuse my Magician Archetype of conjuring an outside-the-box séance.

Or get mercenary and bottle the experience for resale.

Or consort with an analyst to coach me to coerce my Inner Hero to hurl the whole shebang into the Collective Unconscious.

More likely I'll get with the program and declare I've finally and officially landed in California and am getting one facet of the inside view of what all the fuss is about. Here on the legendary ledge. Where only the odd, the outlandish, or the strong, evolve.

Synchronous All Over Again

I arrive in Santa Cruz an aspiring poet fresh from a year living out of a backpack in Hawaii, only to find there is a glut of image gatherers already living here. My sense of living *the* unique West-Coast-Bohemian writer's life is challenged. I learn that many others have beaten me to that castle by a decade or more.

To make matters worse, the poetic language they speak is foreign. My ear hears only sing-song rhymes and so reproduces verbal Norman-Rockwellian knockoffs.

Despite my bruised sense of self, I know I am a poet even though I have yet to discover what that truly entails. A well-informed friend says, "You think you want to write poetry? Take Mort Marcus' course and you'll find out."

On campus, at the first class, a stocky, elegantly-brash, break-the-professor-mold of a literary Goliath enters. He says nothing and writes three words on the board:

MYSTERY. WONDER. VISION.

"This is the essence of poetry," he pronounces. "I know, because I have worked hard to know. If you are able to not simply sit here, but to bring your A game, to be willing to give up your ideas of what poetry is, and to do this persistently until the end of the semester, you may catch a glimpse of knowing."

At that proclamation, fully one-third of the hopefuls sprint for the proverbial door.

The remainder of the classes are held in private homes where we gather, get loaded, get lectured, and write like inspired scribes. When we read however, our poetic egos are succinctly destructed by Mort the Ego Crusher.

One night we have a lesson on using synchronicity as one doorway into bringing a loftier dimension to our poems. In the middle of holding forth, Mort looks up at a picture on the wall of an American Indian involved in dance or ritual. His eyebrows rise a trifle. He tells us that he gave the same lecture to another group two days before. And the *same* painting was on that wall.

On cue, the landlady arrives and leans in from her entry. "Oh, you're having poetry!"

"Yes," says Mort, "Would you honor us with a poem?"

With but two seconds of pause and with a fixed twinkle, she answers, "May your moccasins dance the path that leads you toward the true sky."

Most of us swear the Indian on the wall stifles a laugh.

"There it is again," I blurt.

"There it is again," echoes Mort.

At the Stoplight

I have already accepted that he will be my life-long mentor.

After one of Professor Mort Marcus' evening poetry classes, I pull my pickup to a stop at a light five miles from the college.

I am on a mission to learn the guitar. In fact it's sitting on my lap, stuffed between my stomach and the steering wheel. Inspired by the class, I'm using the hands-free minute to strum out a new verse to the song that's begun to swirl in my head. The images are begging to be coaxed out.

As the light turns green, I glance over at the car next to me only to spot Mort himself writing furiously on a poem then lowering his clipboard. We both hit the gas hoping for the next light to turn red.

American Bridge

From the first time I knew what a bridge was, I needed to build one. As a child, I'd spend hours in sand piles with Lincoln Logs and toy cars building elaborate highways with bridges as centerpieces. In summer, I'd drag the whole menagerie to the beach and growl at people who dared step across the borders of my fantasy zone.

A desire to act out this obsession on the landscape of the larger North American continent propels me through college. That is until the Viet Nam War derails my budding bridge-building vision before it can blossom. After a three-year, defense-job diversion followed by a one-year, early-life-crisis-in-Hawaii detour, in its own way and time, the universe delivers.

My first West-Coast landlady has a small farm served by a bridge fashioned from sagging logs someone had dragged across a chasm and nailed a deck onto. We would literally bargain with the gods every time we crossed the sixty-foot span pleading they would hold it up for one more crossing.

Upon learning I am a closet structural engineer, landlady asks if I would design a sturdy yet affordable replacement for the failing relic. She doesn't need to beg.

Using carrot-juice-powered hippies, we dig the abutments, set forms, place steel, pour concrete, and hand-saw decades-old long beams into curbs, braces and railings. We chant like maniacs to keep the building inspectors away.

On the appointed day, a long semi backs the two main wide-flange beams down toward the creek where twenty-five California crazies wait to hand-lift them onto the backs of trucks then down into place.

Just before I cross the old bridge one last time with one end of the sixty-foot I-beams teetering on my '54 Chevy pickup—and me perched to jump clear and into the chasm should the rotting structure collapse—I spot a fancy red flag hung off the rear end of the big rig which, for my ears only, bellows out in triumph: "American Bridge."

Moon Party at Last Chance Road

Everyone hauls in their own law: peyote smoothies, crates of peaches, bricks of sacred herb, flats of berries, at least twenty dogs, half a hundred drums.

At mid-afternoon I attain overload. Dying slowly from the head down, all but paralyzed. On another day this would be Eden. Where a coastal stream pauses to make an oasis, the whole tribe is skinny-dipping. Or sunbathing in perches on a small cliff amongst the coltsfoot and horsetail. A slice of heaven. But if I take another step I'll stumble into Pluto's dark embrace. A psychic brother tunes in to my trauma.

"It's a healing stream. Immerse yourself and you will be reborn."

So I collapse then crawl from July's furnace to baptize myself in the fern-flanked, sand-bottomed, sun-drenched pool. Within one minute, the head-split is gone. The nausea dissolved. The fever defused. Maybe I passed away to the next realm, but I don't care.

A timeless time later, all retire to the pre-arranged feasting zone at the elegantly bucolic spread of a local couple, famous for their community vision. The food is beyond speech. The variety extreme. The quantity unfathomable.

At sundown, some conspire to make music leap from steel-strings. A savvy player captures breathtaking melodies with tortoise-shell shards. A sister blows into a hollow reed and enchantment births out the other end. A few fiddle on catgut strings which could be tears dancing.

At moonrise it turns full savage. Several troopers start a scrap-wood blaze. The mood goes pagan. Bellies pulse. Dogs do the monkey. One brother blows a gale into a mouth organ. More beat with sticks on ancient-looking hunks of wood. Tambourines erupt as if possessed.

Some open their throats like bawling songbirds. Some swish around the rim drunk on motion, mimicking the dogs. Countless others urge their hands onto the stretched skins of dead cattle. One stands motionless holding crystals aloft.

All leap internally because leaping is the reason for breathing. All embrace this entrapment. Being detained in the moment is a prerequisite to inhaling this rhythmic bliss.

Those toward the epicenter weep. People on the periphery catch the tears and welcome their own inner tremors.

By midnight, our band of crazy saints and runaway angels knows not to ask where the hours-long song came from. The moon-burst sky now plays us too silently for the late arrivals to hear the grateful notes emanating from the spun-out stars we have become.

Up Shasta

I look down only to discover I'm on a sheer-ice cliff with no hope of descending.

My only move is to continue the climb—and hope that the chute doesn't steepen further.

It all seemed so perfectly easy yesterday at the permit office, despite one fateful glitch.

"They're required," says the ranger.

So I force myself to rent the ice crampons, double back and dangle them before the ranger to secure my permit. After he signs me up, I pilot my sun-colored '54 Chevy pickup named "Sky" to the lot at 6500 feet. I toss on my pack and hike in to the crude base camp lodge at 8000 feet.

The sleep there on wire racks with eleven others is oddly alone. We rise in the predawn and break fast in silence like we're taking communion in a dimly-lit church.

In the early light, two miles up, we skirt the campers huddled around the puddling tarn and begin the tedious huff up the infamous, cinder-encrusted heart, a practically vertical black-shrapnel beach where many a fated hiker has lost footing. Sliding then tumbling. Slowly at first, then with a sinister acceleration, finally ending her or his grand dive at some big, immobile, karmic rock, heart forever silenced.

I reach the top of the cinder heart alone at the base of Red Banks, an imposing array of cliffs distinctly visible from the Interstate far below. I assume there is a well-marked trail. Instead I stare at an oddly gay array of flagged sticks stuck into the ice. One of these is planted at the base of a rock-and-ice chute that appears to ascend benignly up and through the cliff face—an arroyo-like shortcut if you will.

It turns out you wouldn't.

And I shouldn't have. After donning the crampons I thought were an overkill joke, and ascending the equivalent of a six-story building, I look down only to discover I'm stuck to the side of an ice cube with no hope of descending.

Instead of renting an ice axe, I have brought my trusty hatchet with which I had attempted to conquer various Hawaiian wildernesses. It has a wooden handle sawed off at a 45-degree angle. I use the handle to claw into the ice while my crampon-assisted feet dig in.

I've become a triangle-shaped, overgrown bacterium suctioned to the side of a petri-dish precipice. A real-time study in the consequences of having taken a wrong turn.

Shouting is futile. Any others are far below. If I don't move I freeze. If I do move I might slip.

So here I dangle—a large icebound parasite who must plan every handhold. Plot every foothold. Gage every weight shift.

Who must hug each jutting rock. Who must urge his whole body to caress the frozen water. Who must wiggle upward with a will which blocks out any thought but achieving the posture of the next wedge. Who must not picture skidding down the chute. Who must not visualize tumbling the length of the hungry heart. Who must not imagine painting what's left of his flesh upon the rigid canvas of some lonesome boulder. Who must delicately catapult his essence inch by inch into that rarified air shared by those who dwell in the stoic strata of non-panic.

Out of the pure silence I hear a slamming noise coming from outside my self. It is a momentary shockwave to discover this to be the hammering of my own heart. I have no doubt that if there are angels, they listen for such things. Like paramedics, they rush to the scene and use their wills to buoy up humans in desperate straits. I whisper some utterance between a plea and a prayer.

A delicious calmness overtakes me. I know where to place my limbs, my torso. I can only conclude we made a deal: my rescue in exchange for telling their story.

After an eternity of minutes, the incline begins to lessen. I spot what can only be flat terrain twenty feet up. I am a silent trumpet playing the most joyous note it will ever play. Just a few more squiggles. A hoist. Now a crawl. And a prolonged shudder as I emerge from the alive end of the deadly white shaft. When I at last regain my feet above the cliff top, a tsunami of gratitude surges through me. To this day, it continues to inundate my soul's every pixel.

I float across a long and blinding snow-carpeted plateau arriving at the small hot pool that saved John Muir's life when he was trapped at this very spot overnight in a storm.

From here the fourteen-thousand-foot summit is still forty stories above. I ascend and write, "This silence is music!" in the register. Then tarry to laugh with the summer-vacationing chipmunk and witness my arms opening to the Holy Land stretched before me, angel-rich and brimming.

From this height one can never descend.

Girl In Charge of Joy

I wonder if, as some claim, there is any Intelligence behind the Big Bang. There are times when it looks as if. The night my daughter was born was one of those. Even though—or because—it was a Caesarian section, she entered the world like royalty soon growing into a sweet California toddler. She loved red shoes and bananas and riding in my truck. Growing up on a farm among goats, chickens, a duck named Ida, and Duster the horse, she was destined to follow her mother's lead and join the next generation of earth-worshiping women. Destined for that and so much more.

For me, her journey starts with one of my unknown ancestors way back in Eastern Europe, probably about the time the first Gypsy entered my bloodline. This aberration at its worst manifested generations of womanizers, wild and maladjusted women, detached alcoholics. And at its best, occasional driven individuals with a distorted urge to excel.

Having inklings of this, I vow to be that one stalwart per generation who breaks the mold. I set about confronting my demons. "I will drain away the inertia of wife batterers. I will transform the hard identity crises of my immigrant forefathers into gentleness toward all. I will provide my daughter with an open-ended destiny. She will be a learner, a teacher, and above all, a beacon. She shall have no limits."

From that ecstatic moment when I hold her for the first time, I see her future in the flood of pictures that begin to inhabit every crevice of my psyche. I know she will outgrow—but never abandon--the earthy roots from whence she springs. We are in awe to witness her intelligence doubling almost daily—in synch with the phenomenon that literally sets humans apart from the rest of the animal kingdom: the tripling of brain size in the first few years of life.

As she grows up in the West Coast counterculture, it is a joy to watch her forays into the magic of color. Easy to watch her internalize the rhythms of the guitars, the banjoes, the woodwinds, the Middle-Eastern strings. Watch her hold up her arms and spin around, eyes closed yet body and mind firmly imbedded in the moment. Upon trying to catch a flitting monarch, we write down her first poem: "See buddy fly!"

Wise people say the explosion of flowers upon the planet coincided with the ascendance of the human species. These gifts were crucial in our evolution. For us, she takes this to new heights: we see her as part calla lily, part Kachina doll, part little woman. A Sacred Trinity.

At the beginning of her second spring, flowers arise early and prolific. These daily child-flower encounters are magical to witness. The variety of colors and aromas unlock her senses. In turn, floods of questions arise. All would be answered from the point of view of the deep magic her parents know to be afoot both on the farm and in the larger world.

But lest we forget, destiny is the operative force in play here. Of course she would begin to illustrate the perfect blend of sensory experience and intellect. Of course she is running a dreamlike and color-filled race through grade school. Like a normal child, she would try to vault over obstacles seen and unseen only to fall off her bike and crack a rib. Or break open a knee. Or wound her pride.

You can see the grounding start to unfold in her. (The world reveals its pains and terrors to most of us in dosages we can absorb, perhaps preparing us for the larger ones.)

It would appear that she discovers poetry in junior high, but I swear to you, I watch as poetry discovers her. I say this without shame or boast, for the Muse has taught me to look through his lens at the exchanges afoot in this earthly domain. Like her father, she falls hard for algebra and trig. "It's so cool! So exact. Such a tool. What kind of work uses it? Good. I want to do that."

Though it is tempting, I can't portray her as perfect. Her struggles through high school would fill several novels. Like sneaking out of her window and staying out all night. Getting caught with weed. Two boys fighting because of her. She would laugh cruelly until it dawns on her one summer day that love is what it's all about. I can only walk the sidelines of her world reduced to invoking some form of divine intervention. I would shout encouragement onto her playing field but the words are blocked by the boisterous game. Wiser people than I would simply offer, "Welcome again and again to parenthood."

Senior year, in full womanly regalia for the prom, as she hugs me and disappears with her date, that attached piece of me begins the perishing that every parent fears. No amount of foreknowledge prepares one for the bottom dropping out of his universe. Surely some cruel gnome has lulled me into believing she would never grow out of the life we gave her. A home, her room, the coaches, the community. This departure can certainly be postponed. Something will freeze time. Stop the inevitable.

Her first substantive call from college makes me wish I could reverse my age, disguise myself, and experience her experience as some sort of peer—not as some far-away bystander with a checkbook. "God Dad, my mind is so stimulated! I want to know everything about everything. Thank you for saving the money to send me to this awesome place. Uh oh. Got band practice. Gobs of homework. Gotta go! Love you."

It really is as Gibran says: "You may house their bodies but not their souls. For their souls dwell in the house of tomorrow, which you cannot visit, not even in your dreams."

"Hi Dad, is there a way I can spend my junior year abroad?"

Doesn't she want to enjoy us? Are we that out of it? We're still cool...whatever that means. And if we're not, we'll take classes. Yes, as you may suspect, the "we" is not her birth mother and me. There's that destiny card again. The "we" is her stepmom and me. Two flowers in our own right blooming in a new garden. But a beat would never be missed in our home when it comes to loving her unconditionally.

We cry with her when the scholarship to grad school falls through and she has to pull herself together. When she falls hard for her first big love and he says he's not ready. When she lands the job that would come to define her early adulthood.

This heart-rending, heart-enhancing love prompts me to proclaim that providing her start in life fundamentally changed me. Altered forever my outlook on the undeniable preciousness of a child's life.

If she were in my presence now, I imagine her saying, "Papa, where are all my pictures? I can't find them anywhere."

So I ask you, go back in this story to where the tense of my verbs wavers from present to conditional progressive. Go back to the beginning of her second spring. Back to that time when we all were innocent. And know that though her sweet, not quite two-year-old life was snuffed out, summoning her imagined future has set me adrift on an even deeper reservoir of joy. I must trust that this continues to be her special mission. The ultimate coincidence in a father's journey. Ordained from the moment the Big Bang flowered.

DAUGHTERS

Among many books, we look through *Technicians of the Sacred* for clues to the name of our new daughter. We find a poem by a squaw named Moki whose name means "Little Woman" in the Cheyenne tongue. This seems right as our child's mother's name is Cheyenne. We have been calling her "Little Spirit" from the time she was conceived. Both her parents having changed their names, we decide she should help choose hers. One day when we know she understands enough language, we start playfully throwing out names. When we say, "Moki" she says, "Moki." Because she looks like a Kachina doll, we say, "Moki Kachina!" and without any hesitation she shouts, "Yeah! Moki 'Cheena!"

This occurs on day 333 of her existence and so becomes her name. On her six hundred forty-first afternoon, she crawls under a pickup as her mother and a friend converse. They forget to account for her as the truck is slipped into reverse. She returns to the spirit realm after a very quick transit through our lives. As her mother and I had separated not long before, I receive the news in Calgary and fly to Mexico to grieve with cherished friends in the heated stream where Pancho Villa hid out. I too hide there and re-emerge with a scar to cover the gash on my soul.

Allow me to speak about the scar. Its tissue is laden with indelible imprints. Her room-filling smile. Her little red shoes. Her lovingly-built crib. Her love of bananas. The scar's tissue is ripe with sounds I will hear for eternity. "Papa! Papa! Need diaper!...Papa, please. Want just a coupl'a dates."

The scar begins to heal four years later when my hands catch my second daughter entering the world in a mountain cabin from the womb of another chosen mother on April Fool's Day. That midnight we take her outside. She smiles at the moon. So we name her Maluna. This too seems right as her father's name is Sun and her mother's name is Star. A celestial family. But, as if destined to experience the emptiness of outer space, Star shoots off into alien ethers, leaving me adrift once more. Fifteen years after her cosmic birth, the moonchild orbits around to the backside of a stray asteroid and becomes eclipsed from me. I lose sight of her for nine trying years. It feels like another version of death. Except this one is superseded by a rebirth which begins on a sunlit, flowery street in the City of Angels.

It can be dangerous to explore the symbolisms that enrich our lives. One focuses on them at his or her peril. Walking this path will be at times fatiguing, at times exhilarating and almost always tedious to those we touch—especially loved ones. The vistas along the way give glimpses into a parallel realm designed to tease, to enrich, to torment. Often these happen singularly, sometimes all at once, always intensely.

I have bet my life their covert purpose is to awaken us to our God-selves. To co-create with Designer. To honor Creator as Poet, Artist, Comedian, Madman. To discover God as Relentless Remindor that our boundaries on the earth plane are imaginary. To revel in our swim in the pool of human experience: the joys, the griefs, the shocks, the rewards, the inescapable lessons, the momentary euphorias, even the often faint yet steady rumble of the Reaper's unstoppable strut.

If our motion through life is on a path, a boulevard, or a highway, the symbols and synchronicities represent trail markers, yield signs, mileposts. So let them reveal to us where we are on the journey. Let them lead us to that fuel which propels us to the next shelter, next lane change, next merge—and on to the final off ramp.

Sweat Without End

Several men coil into the hut. Its floor is earth, the odor holy.

Fiery rocks are brought on a metal shovel until the bit blisters. The sun has singed my skin though I am noticeably white beneath.

> *"For those of you who've never sweated*
> *this is about all our people have left.*
> *Almost everything else has been taken."*

Our fireman closes the flap and I, knifed to nothing by the quick dark, expire into a greater mind to recognize this light of Red Nation igniting my insides is more alive than thought itself.

And there are details I cannot give. Meanings unsealed by the steam I must not refine. Words I find myself singing I did not know before.

This is a place for pray-ers and I re-embrace the power of that medium.

This is sweat too intense to remember—except the end of Red Cloud's confession:

> *"And sometimes I struggle grandfather*
> *for I have been taught an Indian is first*
> *an individual yet one who receives strength*
> *from his nation people grandfather.*
> *One who owes strength to his nation people."*

This is sweat too intense to remember—except the edge of Mohawk's lament:

> *And grandfather I pray for the whites*
> *I hear they once had tribes grandfather.*
> *They are now confused grandfather."*

AIM Encampment
Point Conception, 1978

Stop the Musical

I embrace my bucolic karma and dwell on one of the funkiest farms on the West Coast. The main house fights for its life against termites, rot, and hillside creep. There is a garden we carved and terraced onto a slope rife with gophers and voles shunted by a digging dog. An arbor that sags from years of grunting against the full-bunch succulence of prolific purple grapes. A barn held up by bowed braces, rusted hardware, concrete substitute and a large dose of momentum.

Our cabin is that faded red that infects the mind's palette with melancholy from bygone eras. It perches high over a goat pen at the bottom of a slanting pasture where a dusty horse lets us ride her bare back.

We are gods whose limits are unknown to ourselves. Most nights we sweat like devils in a wood-fired sauna just off the jumbo plastic pool—six feet deep at the middle—complete with a rigged waterfall whispering onto it off the top of the arbor.

This is the quintessential hippie picture: elegant peasant on a budget with pantries of canned fruit, bins of homemade compost, an outdoor stage where we rehearse songs and skits to counteract the reckless money-changers who spoil the greater habitat.

But one January night a bingeing storm overfills the round pool. The ensuing waterspout surges forth, in turn collapsing the rock wall that holds up the slope below. Mud and rocks slog across the driveway and kiss up hard against my trusting cabin. The tremor jars me from my writer's trance. I force the door open only to gape at the spilling-over pool twenty feet above, savagely undermining the rest of its own foundation.

Within seconds, a grinding sound gives just enough warning to run as the huge pool converts its whole two-thousand-cubic-foot volume to a giant wave which hits the unsuspecting cabin, launching it like a midget Titanic, way beyond the bleating goats seventy feet into the horse pasture.

The next morning I enter the mostly-intact cabin in search of the last penned words of the two-act musical farce I was bringing to life last night. My desk is on the down-slope side of the structure and has landed with papers a bit water-anointed—but miraculously intact—on the writing surface.

I find my still-uncapped pen dormant over the top paper, the last lines of which, I swear by all that is sacred, read:

Hey diddle diddle, hey diddle ditch
The Plan presents: The Water Witch

Freeway Scream

When I find out the last several months have been a lie, I drive screaming down the freeway. There is one scream in particular that is so soul-wrenching I am thrust into another dimension. A place where the pain that propelled me here drops away like the spent stage of a booster rocket momentarily exposing my core to be a vast vortex lined with euphoria yet allowing every known emotion to swirl within it.

I find myself at once in awe of the design of the human experience. Its terrible depth. Its mostly inaccessible power. Its elusive, impermanent, ever-available joy.

A few months before, she had said she was going over to a girlfriend's for the evening. An hour after she left I became suddenly dizzy, blinded and disoriented. I wobbled to the couch doubling over because I could no longer stand. Like fainting without losing consciousness. I found if I shook my head violently, my vision would clear for a second or two. Then the sense of my body aliveness departing—coupled with a black brightness instead of vision—would resume.

I thought I might be dying.

In its own way it is a death. Finding out these months later that she was in bed at that moment with my best friend and musical partner, triggers this soul- plagued sound. All of the intricate bonds of the three of us are forever severed. Hence the profound scream which allows the exorcism of those bonds.

I can only conclude that the force behind betrayal is intense and grave. It is akin to dying—both for the betrayer and the betrayed. It is deeply, terrifyingly human. And to be human is sometimes joyously, sometimes tragically, yet always inescapably—mystifying.

Kaiser Pass Primal Love

Our fondness is tentative: two love-hungry predators circling each other. My daughter, her son, and we two would-be lovers ascend a pass on the western Sierra slope, heading for lakes and trails and hot springs.

Rain throbs. The air thins. An American Indian rock and roll band wailing, "Christopher Columbus, what have you done to us?" has us fully jacked up.

On our ascent, it's as if some power beyond me turns the steering wheel of the van aiming it down an unmarked dirt road. The track doesn't really end so much as expand onto a pasture. Several serene cows are in attendance.

We'll never be able to—nor should we dare—explain this force that launches all of us hollering onto the meadow.

"O my God, there's a dead cow!"

We are already half jogging. But now the three-year old, the five-year old and the tentative lovers begin racing and screaming around and around the fallen cow. Feeding off one another but mostly off the massive deceased bestial apparition in the wet meadow. Amid lightning and thunder and alpine-scented air.

She looks at me and is the first to know that this is wild—and therefore true—love. Some men are slower. I feel but a medium-level twinge.

We re-enter the van and vault over the summit to a basin where, suddenly becoming an uncaged bird, she darts from the rig, lunges onto a sapphire lake, and swims like a swan across its expanse.

Now am I smitten.

The wildness of that force has never left us.

Rebirth by Fire

The smoke alarm—the one I'd replaced the batteries in seven weeks earlier— blasts its panicked drone into my brain.

Eight weeks ago, before my and my new girlfriend's first big trip together, I make a safety check. This includes replacing those batteries.

I have no clue this simple adult act will save my life.

While in Mexico, we buy a cache of hand-woven carpets in Oaxaca. We set out to peddle them at the upscale Marin flea market, the morning after enjoying a feral night on Mt Tam.

The well-to-do are not only not impressed by our afterglow, they communicate it by not buying. We return late, exhausted from the psychic fencing, she to her bungalow, me to the mountain house where the smoke detectors lie dormant yet vigilant. Well into the wee hours, they assert their authority, eventually rousing me from a deep pre-workaday dream laced with the noise of hammer drills and power saws.

It is a strange event to watch my painstakingly built home burn in the rear view mirror after breaking a window with my bare hand to get a hose into the room that is smoldering. I break the window letting oxygen rush in. Using the hand severs tendons in my wrist. A wall of fire explodes in my face. Strange because in my middle-of-the-night fumbling, I contribute to the home's demise.

In an odd and ominous way, the fire prompts a friend to scold me: "Rebuild this home to be a reflection of your consciousness; an artwork worthy of your vision."

It takes twenty-eight more years to perfect the canvas: eleven levels, fifteen exterior stone stairways, four hundred tons of slate placed in walls and floors one piece at a time, banana trees bearing in the solarium, reams of copper for the roofs, enough reclaimed redwood to re-start a forest.

After this long-dreamed conclusion, only three weeks later we move out. As I pilot the last load of possessions down the driveway, the same voice that has escorted me through every joy-pain step, eggs out one more refrain: "If you can't enjoy each mini victory, each distinct completion, every errand, every last driven screw and puttied nail, go find another universe. This one is designed to bless you with the gifts of strength through setbacks, motion despite exhaustion, and fleeting elegance as a by-product of sheer will. But only if you've courted Lady Luck and honored Mother Earth."

The Great Image Heist

The southern Spanish coast in July is ruled by herds of humans. Hostels run out of rooms and rent tents. Discos overflow, hotels groan, even beaches dream of breathing room. Mother, father, son—plus luggage—drive west in a small red car in ninety-degree heat quenching our already inundated spirits with glimpses of the aquamarine sea.

We'd come from spending three point three days in the sea riding wind-swell waves from Africa on a cape named on behalf of cats. We'd toured a cave where Neanderthals played house. We'd feasted like queen, king and prince felines on the resident fish. Now even the road-provoked sweat adds potency to this Mediterranean tableau.

Halfway back to a disco town where our teenage son aimed to cavort, we spot an emerald edged beach that calls to us like a Siren. This seems seductively synchronistic since the Pillars of Hercules are just a discus throw down the road. In other words, we turn off for a swim in the aura of the Rock of Gibraltar.

As a child, I'd fallen in love with tunnels. I'd beg my parents to drive hundreds of miles off course so I could be thrilled by their inherent daring. Tunnels for me have always been mystical. And so it is to be with the one we find ourselves in on the approach to the beach. It is cut through the ancient rock for a quarter mile, yet wide enough to stow cars inside.

It has water dripping from its ceiling. It sports a miniature bay at one end and jagged Spanish cliffs on the other. And it is as cool in here as the inside of a pint of peach sorbet.

Rather than park in the noon fever, we squeeze the stunted car into the middle of the tunnel and sashay toward the aqueous expanse. Oddly, my family watches me swim alone, an orphaned dolphin forgetting his story as it dissolves in the gently-scented sea.

A short, but euphoric quarter hour later, we retreat to the tunnel to find our red car emptied of all the luggage, all the clothes, all the gear, all the rare Moroccan souvenirs; even my newly-rendered dental clinic design for a poverty-afflicted village in Ghana. And especially my folder chocked with every poem I'd hoped to hone, every image I'd longed to prolong; every unfinished stanza to whose cravings I'd been listening for years. Night and day they have called out: *"Display us. Don't let us languish in your files. Please. Display our lush, linguistic, big-headed behavior before it's too late!"*

In the flick of a criminal's quick decision, it has suddenly become too late.

My son and I race up and down the highway but the trail goes quickly cold in the 100-degree heat. The local police gallantly refuse to put out a bulletin for a street-wise, guilty-as-sin, English-as-a-second-language bandit showing off my sky-colored, silk chemise. He can't be that hard to spot, high as he is on sniffing our elixir-rich wardrobe, slathering his face with our expired sunscreen, all the while leaving a trail of guttural commotion as he ingests my poetry.

But somewhere in his twisted spirit he knows I'm after him. Over his shoulder he hallucinates I'm a block behind him in Barcelona. He's convinced I'm spying him through binoculars from a tower at the Alhambra. He hears me rustling the shrubs on the other side of his wall. He swears I've tapped his phone. He's certain the next time he turns his car key, he'll be blown piecemeal to some stadium in Hades where the ghosts of slain bulls are waiting to trample what's left of him.

For my part, at a packed outdoor café, I creep up to the crowd's edge. Pretend to look on in awe as he enthralls his audience, inviting them in a collective jog around Saturn's bracelets. I force a smile as he stands at the podium, saddles an imaginary stallion, and canters it through a canyon so ancestral that waterfowl fly in living petroglyphs. I politely applaud as he bows after reciting an infusion of fire so passionate the immediate city is endangered All the while I seethe, "This is *my* jogging track, *my* stallion, *my* waterfowl, *my* fire danger."

Then I look from his contorted mouth to his void-like eyes and say, "Brother your taste in poetry is rivaled only by your ability to thieve treasures from trusting tourists while they frolic in your sea as innocents who believed their world was free of local leeches trying to suck the positive charge from their unsuspecting blood."

Then, realizing I am becoming him and horrified at that outcome, I cuff us together, lug us to that tunnel, and with the social herd there present as our witness, vow to recite our grievances to the Almighty Air and profess our allegiance to the Great Generosity, so that one small crevice in the slippery cliff of hatred may, in the end, be erased forever from the southern coast of Spain, basecamp of certain direct descendants of the Neanderthals.

Presence Circle

There is nothing more to investigate at this spiritual mountain outpost run by a sundry cluster of American Hindus, on a Saturday night at the pinnacle of a six-day retreat led by a renegade, Australian, non-dual, be-in-the-moment master.

It's futile to reflect on how and why our particular pack of seekers has arrived at this state where the self-distorted stories of our lives are best left out in the hallway pleading with our limp coats and empty shoes to listen to them.

Ninety of us sit in a circle each with a partner directly across on an imaginary line through the center. We fall silent into an ever-unfolding moment.

My partner's visage becomes Indian squaw, then brave, then Shinto priest, then Apache chief with headdress, then Mongolian tribesman, then herself, then others too fast to absorb. A potent past-life Rolodex? A group-induced mirage? A parting of the veil that cloaks the divine?

After the circle disperses, in our unspoken oath of silence we overhear the Ego resume its duty to sap the intent of this vision by injecting us with random mental debris. But like a welcome flood, we overhear the silence of the ever-available moment expose and submerge these cheap seductions.

We overhear the vastness. We fight the urge to label it—and lose. God. Great Mystery. The One. The Word. We're human after all and one of our strongest cravings is to try to make sense of the infinite. So we label.

We might overhear the Apostle, Paul writing to the Ephesians about "…how the mystery was made known to me by revelation…"

We might overhear The Buddha say, "Whatever precious jewel there is in the heavenly worlds, there is nothing comparable to one who is Awakened."

Or overhear Proverbs declare, "It is the glory of God to conceal a thing; but the glory of kings to search it out…"

Later if we were to compare notes, we'd affirm that Grace Slick and the Jefferson Airplane were onto a cosmic truth when they proclaimed: "You are the Crown of Creation—and you've got no place to go!"

To carry the metaphor forward, when we immerse ourselves in the Nectar of Now, Creation wears each of *us* as its ultimate crown at long last.

Over New Mexico

She is reading like a fiend on the plane over New Mexico. I doze off and when I stir she pounces.

"You've got to read this paragraph!" she says, thrusting her book in my vision.

I absorb the eloquent passage.

"It's good," I say. "Inspiring even. It has a magical, kind of surreal yet grounded quality. Who wrote it?"

"Isabel Allende."

"Wait a minute. Look at this," I offer.

On my lap is a tattered handout of short poems, stories and articles I had dragged home from a writing workshop perhaps a decade before. Last night while packing—at the last minute as usual—I'd unearthed this treasure from one stack of many in my cluttered office. I turn to one of the Xeroxed pages I'd read just before dozing off and hand it to her.

It's a brief treatise on magical realism by none other than… Isabel Allende!

"These events you call mystical—nothing special," she scowls, as if in resonance for landing in skeptical New York. "Not amazing. Not synchronistic. Just common coincidence."

I look out the window, down at New Mexico. Land of Enchantment. Land of Magical Realism. Same thing.

You decide.

Celestial Timing

Forty-five thousand years ago, all but a thin crescent of a great round island collapsed into the Mediterranean. Precipitous cliffs remain where the land sheared away violently.

Just now, the early afternoon sun penetrates the sea creating a hue so immensely cerulean, so planetarily rare, that as I snorkel above the abyss, surely I look directly into the third eye of the Creator.

The whole of the remaining island is imbued by—and wedded to—the seemingly bottomless caldera, which lends the environs an inbuilt cosmic dose of depth so deep it approaches oneness.

This atmosphere brings a surge of grace into my pen-weary fingers.

The pen's journey starts forty years back, when a friend invites me to his attic for an experiment. He had composed a piano score for the moon, the sun, and each of the planets. "While I meditate, record your impressions. Translate them if you will, into poems praising each celestial body."

The acceptable first drafts take eight years. Two years after that, several newly-revised sketches are lost when my house burns to the ground. Several of the poems are stubborn and argue with me for over a decade. Finally in Costa Rica sixteen years downstream of the attic, two more—Uranus and Neptune—allow themselves to be revealed. The next morning, while I am out enjoying some river-mouth waves, a thief steals into the car and heists my briefcase. I hear echoes of those poems laughing all the way to his never-to-be discovered hut.

At eighteen years downstream of the attic, another thief gets three more in Spain from a car we'd parked in a tunnel at a beach on the Costa del Sol. Along with every last bag, basket, and suitcase.

The wait for this Santorini surge has taken another nine years. It has not been a graceful wait. The cumulative loss is like having one of my heart chambers removed while I sleep.

But when I land here on Santorini my spirit begins to tingle. I jump yelling off a cliff into aquamarine tonic. Above the abyss with the local teens. All of us addicts of the unknown. The metaphor does not escape me. Back in the room, I can't scribble the unknown whispers and shouts of certain planets fast enough.

Seven burned, twice-stolen poems are spontaneously re-hydrated. The solar system springs to warmth within me—again. Neptune, Uranus, Jupiter re-emerge from sleep.

But like the orbits of the planets themselves, the poems now revolve in a seldom-visited file. A file that has survived one fire, two thefts, and three hard-drive crashes. I have an odd knowing that when they so dictate, they will emerge from the decades-long shadow of their current eclipse and scintillate.

BEING ON THE GURNEY

In a prolonged moment lying on a stainless steel gurney surrounded by plant-colored walls and white uniformed staff moving around me like untroubled clouds in a hospital hallway on a San Francisco hill where I wait for a second operation on my shattered femur by a revered Israeli surgeon all the while aware of the possibility of not reawakening from the anesthetic into this world, yet there is also transmitted a palpable, inaudible, transparent music which is so extremely calming I actually remember that if I can be with the walls, the cloud beings, even the ceiling tiles, even the IV draining into my body (some charmed fluid my soul has probably pre-approved) then why not just accept everything and say, "Life, I am willing to let go of you because this moment you've designed is more than enough."

Mile 232 Rapid

Still wet from capsizing my inflatable kayak in mile 231 Rapid, I scout 232 with the others. The sight of it makes my blood freeze.

The guide says, "Go just right of the top hole, ride those two huge standing waves, then bust hard left to miss that rock chute. If you eat it, swim hard to the center. Swim for your life! Bad juju in the chute!"

I enter last—after the four oar boats and the crazy boys in the double inflatable. I'm a helpless twig, at the mercy of the accelerating current. I skirt past the hole and sit atop each of the two waves, upright and in control.

"Ridin' the big dogs!" I yell. But while I'm busy congratulating myself, I miss the window at which to paddle left for my life, an unrecoverable three seconds go by. I look downstream to find I'm closing like a maniac on the jutting rock that forms the left side of the chute. "Swim for your life!" still hanging in the ether above the thundering rapid now ricochets through me as a shriek.

So I make a split-second decision to exit the kayak, pushing off hard and diving for the center of the mighty and roaring Colorado with the warning, "Avoid the chute at all costs!" still lodged in my ears.

But the current has other ideas. I am sucked under—feet first—and, unbeknownst to me, funneled spread-eagle through the forbidden chute, miraculously avoiding the submerged spire jutting up in the middle of that narrow water alley. Both ends of the paddle I am still clutching bump rock as in a pinball game. A human thread passing through the eye of a jagged needle.

I pop up fifty feet below the chute to discover I had taken the road through hell. My commander-less kayak had taken the safe route in the center of the river.

Part of me celebrates, grateful for the angel that guarded my passage.

Part of me remains there, submerged. In the eye. Paddle bumping rock. Spread out like the Holy Ghost. Face down. Inches above the knifelike spire. Almost sliced.

Better part than all.

The Adoption

My beloved, non-blood-related son of nearly two decades returns from a deep state in Israel with a long list of interactions to accomplish. He asks his mother and me to accompany him to some large rocks on our neighborhood Northern California beach.

He pulls out some carefully-prepared documents he's generated in longhand and presents them to me.

This is one of those moments on the journey where time doesn't just stand still. The participants have been ushered into a side room by magnanimous beings where the very idea of a clock—not to mention the wall it would have been mounted upon—is superseded by an elixir of psychoactive remedies and organic grace.

With his mother (my wife) signing as witness, the papers are a pact between us that I adopt him as my son and he adopts me as his father. All speak in the hallowed tongue of affirmation, joyfully sign, and inhale deeply of the sweet and saline Pacific air. As court adjourns, we brush away some well-earned tears and stroll home knowing that time will have its way with us but this day we have co-created unspeakable, unending beauty for as long as the rocks exist.

Twenty Fourteen Doesn't Speak—It Rages

I rise to contact the eyes of a wife who ages by growing younger. Together we kneel beside sister ocean who is on another of her giving sprees: a shabby chic carpet of cormorants; throngs of martyred anchovies; choruses of sea-lions who clear their throats with the rhythm of an a cappella choir.

In the afternoon, whales erupt out the window. The view from our thirty-year anniversary nest is breathtaking.

A friend stops by for cereal and grieving. Later on a walk to the promontory, wall-to-wall pelicans and gulls sweeten the sea like wind-strewn orchid petals.

The next morning, a local sage races his bicycle through the fog into the next dimension. I attend a concrete pour and pray hard as the gravel is entombed.

Fire Breathers in the bush howl that the President can do nothing suitable even when he's elegantly correct. Pundits splay themselves on each other's forked tongues. Protestors throw body and spirit on the great gears even as the machine outscreams them.

Prisoners get religion. Some get proven innocent. In Texas they get death. Far outside the clang of the gates, the faithful apply extra layers of bandages to their knees all to postpone the inevitable.

Buddhists propose antidotes to the Building Code. Clients specialize in elegantly coarse forms of mental torture. Hindus assume responsibility for everyone. Atheists become unbelievably disillusioned. The Religious Right are busted for ongoing voyeurism.

A father's daughter glances off a wild Dutchman who shines like a newly-minted, single-issue, gold doubloon. Long after the gold tarnishes, she still shimmers with impossible radiance.

A mother's son rides the ancient waves emanating from the Western Wall all the way onto that hallowed sand near where a kindred Abraham freed the slaves.

Up the mountain we hope for a cougar to eat the noxious, noise-breeding roosters, turkeys, sheep, goats, ducks and alpacas the neophyte neighbor raises up like a proxy middle finger. Fear and loathing in the hills at the end of the road reaches a new normal. Hell has heaven in a hammerlock.

The People's Advocate reaches even deeper than the Founders into his medicine pouch. He smokes and smudges the Constitution with sacred herbs to revitalize the root of benevolent intensity from which it sprung. His incantations alter the course of history.

The Landlady paraphrases the stars: *"Dicey is the new normal."*
The Centenarian Matriarch declares: *"The weather has fallen overboard. People are not far behind."*

The Spiritual Tutor transmits the last word:

"All ideas are invalid. All thoughts are untrue. All concepts are contrived. Opinions are not worth the synapses they're firing. Beliefs are out of the question. Only poems born of eternal nothingness are worthy."

The Grandkids

They come out of the Magellanic clouds sprung forth from some upstart planet where laughter *is* the atmosphere.

They don't so much as *learn* to crawl, rather crawling arises within them. You soon discover they've arrived fully equipped with puppet strings worked by tag teams of rabbits and alligators.

When they finally arise and walk, it's as if the whole planet wobbles.

From the very first time they talk words to you in that precious-jewel voice, they have your number and they know it.

They don't actually mimic primitive humans, rather those ancients wander again through them.

Soon and later and most likely ongoingly, they will come to challenge your tranquility. Your stamina. Your intellect. Your world view.

But for now, you cannot contain the elation infecting your every cell with congratulation. For you have succeeded at the board game called Beyond-Your-Self.

You don't so much win the game. Rather you have to admit you must have rigged it knowing your heartstrings would need these many tugs to bring you all the way into that full-soul joy which suspends you—*their* willing puppet—among that riotous gaggle of untamed and tender humanity known as grandkids.

Me   Rilke   Angels

The radio announcer says *authority* at the same moment I read it on the sign out the windshield. This happens with numbers—and many other words—too often to ignore.

I move from town to the hills the morning after a freak wind storm downs a large weeping willow in the front yard. I struggle carrying my things through the downed branches, to drive out to a farm in the Soquel hills. This odd word is the name of the tribe who inhabited the valley where the creek of the same name flows. The word literally means willow, so named for the trees along the creek. I observe that the tree fell exactly in the direction of the Soquel farm as the crow flies.

Almost every time my wife dreams about some acquaintance she's not seen in months or years she runs into them the next day. It seems normal in a cosmically logical sort of way. Notice that *cosmically* and *comically* are very close. Is this God playing practical jokes?

Every few days I glance toward a clock at some significant moment and it reads 11:11. I still own the house whose numbers started out as 1111—the one that burns to the ground and is reborn as 2001. This could be read as "2000 ones"—which when lined up make 500 sets of eleven-elevens. A lifetime supply. My daughter's lucky number is

1111 because it keeps recurring in her life at random and meaningful moments. Certainly because she was born at that address.

My wife's client tells her about a radio show she just heard while driving in. All about the number 1111. Channel surfing, she tuned in just as 11:11 came up on the clock on her dash. My wife counsels the client to embrace the magic.

My last official night in California—after the going-away-party guests have left—I fall into bed and check the cellphone clock: 11:11 of course.

Perhaps these are the ways angels communicate with us. For their amusement.

The poet Ranier Maria Rilke was visited by an angel in a castle by the sea. It spoke to him after which he wrote:

> *"For beauty's nothing but the start of terror we can hardly bear,*
> *and we adore it because of the serene scorn*
> *it could kill us with. Every angel's terrifying."*

Perhaps. But what if we embrace—no, dare to dance with—this brand of angel, heel to toe, bosom to bosom, lip to cheek? Even if the most reductionist version is true—that they are constructs of our higher selves—surely they were wished into existence to more than amuse. They are like the white stones Hansel dropped so he and Gretel might find the way home.

About the Author

William Climbing Sun is a world traveler, engineer, teacher, and poet who now relishes the warm waves in Boca Raton, Florida after savoring four decades in Santa Cruz County, California.

www.ingramcontent.com/pod-product-compliance
Lightning Source LLC
Chambersburg PA
CBHW030004050426
42451CB00006B/111